This journal belongs to

_____
_____
_____
_____
_____
_____

©2018 Stylized Workbooks - All rights reserved.

All rights reserved. No part of this publication may be reproduced, distributed, or transmitted in any form or by any means, including photocopying, recording, or other electronic or mechanical methods, without the prior written permission of the publisher, except in the case of brief quotations embodied in critical reviews and certain other noncommercial uses permitted by copyright law.

For permission requests contact: info@stylizedworkbooks.com

Check out our catalog at

STYLIZEDWORKBOOKS.COM

Printed in France by Amazon
Brétigny-sur-Orge, FR

26079202R00070